The Table of Truth

THE TABLE OF TRUTH

JACOB M. CARTER

WordCrafts

The Table of Truth
Copyright © 2018
Jacob M. Carter

Cover design by Pete Orta

All rights reserved. No part of this book may be reproduced, stored in a retrieval system, or transmitted in any form or by any means – electronic, mechanical, photocopy, recording, or otherwise – without the prior written permission of the publisher. The only exception is brief quotations for review purposes.

Published by WordCrafts Press
Cody, WY 82414
www.wordcrafts.net

Contents

Dedication	vii
Preface	ix
Chapter 1	1
Chapter 2	5
Chapter 3	7
Chapter 4	10
Chapter 5	13
Chapter 6	16
Chapter 7	19
Chapter 8	22
Chapter 9	24
Chapter 10	27
Chapter 11	30
Chapter 12	37
Having It Both Ways	39
Chapter 13	43
Chapter 14	46
Chapter 15	49
Chapter 16	55
In Closing	60
Acknowledgments	63
About the Author	65

Dedication

This book is dedicated to my everyone who has helped me in my journey throughout the last eight years. Each of you have been an instrumental in making me the man that I am today. I hope you are proud of how far the Lord has brought us in such a short amount of time.

Soli Deo Gloria

Preface

In my last book about the Kennedy assassination, **Before History Dies,** I interviewed some of the top experts in the field to give younger people a primer for studying his assassination. I used this format because I thought giving my audience evidence from all sides of the table was important. This generation, my generation, aren't built to simply believe information because you or I do. As a matter of fact, they despise that form of education. That's why I knew it was crucial to not withhold any researcher's opinion, whether I personally agreed with it or not. I had to let them choose for themselves, and I believe they appreciated that format because it gave them the freedom to learn without having to come to the same conclusion that others have.

I did face criticism though. Some older researchers had warned me about the JFK research community beforehand, but I wasn't prepared for how deep the rabbit hole actually spiraled. The criticism, I believe, was unfounded and rooted in traditionalism and bias. There was nothing wrong with my book. I had been as fair and balanced as any JFK author out there. I allowed the conspiracy believers to be represented by their top dogs and I did the same for the lone assassin community. This wasn't enough for some, because it didn't fit into their presupposed worldview. Sure, I wrote a book about the Kennedy assassination that was targeted at getting younger people involved in the case, but I didn't do it their way and that wasn't acceptable.

Many times, I was asked why I had this or that researcher in my book. Why would I allow a guy who believed Oswald acted alone in my book? Why would I put a conspiracy theorist in my book? Why didn't I choose a side? Well, as I stated above, I did it because I understand how to communicate to the people in my age group.

We live in a post-modern world. We don't live in the 1960s anymore. Younger people aren't interested in how much someone knows about a topic as much as they are interested in the authenticity of the individual who's delivering that knowledge. We don't take "sides." We're not black and white in our thinking. We live in the grey areas. We aren't afraid of hearing the other side of a case. As a matter of fact, we are suspicious of those who refuse to show it to us.

Knowing that, I had to change some things up. I realized some older researches might not understand that, but I couldn't write a book to appease their style if I wanted to move this case forward. Reform is hardly ever absent of conflict, but the push back proves the reform is necessary.

Which brings me to this book and why I'm writing it. There are things in the JFK research community that need to be addressed in a book format. As the hype for 2017 builds up in the media, the vitriol and division between researchers is growing as well. The online back biting and gossip between assassination experts isn't helping this case. We aren't in the spirit of JFK when we aren't passing our torch of knowledge to younger people. We can't pass it on if we're only concerned with surrounding ourselves with those who agree what we believe to be true about this case. We also can't do it if we are consumed in gossip. I mean, who really cares what comes out in those October files if we don't have anyone to pass that information onto? What will happen to this case if researchers continue to devour one another through personal attacks? Who's going to pick up the torch if the flame has been quenched?

We can't be fooled. Those files are very important to this case, but so are the points I'm about bring up in this book. The JFK research community needs to be revamped and we're running out of time. I know this won't be easy to hear, and I'm sure further criticism will ensue, but sometimes the truth is more important than being liked. I don't mean to offend anyone or to provoke people into not liking me. But I also can't sit by and allow crime to happen without sounding the alarm. Trust me, that would be the easier path, but I care to much about this time in history to let it fade away into Facebook groups.

There will be some who won't want to change. These are the researches who aren't in this case with pure motives. Maybe they started out with the right mindset, but over a period of years this case has become their identity and they would rather die than give up their JFK research throne. Now, there are tons of researchers who are older than me that I respect and admire. I put many of them in my previous book. But there also are some older researchers who are hurting this case with their refusal to listen and keep adapting with the times. I hope I never become like that myself.

Then there are some who are apathetic. Who cares right? You do you and I'll do me and we'll stay in our lanes to avoid confrontation. They would scoff at a book like this and write it off as idealistic. "No younger person wants to listen" they say. "There's no point." On the contrary my friends, I know the fatalists are wrong because I was able to get them to listen by speaking in their language and refusing to get personal. After all, if my goal is to educate younger people about the importance of this case then I shouldn't wait till they care. I should try to tell them why they should care. It's simple laziness, or a lack of conviction, if we aren't willing to invest in someone until we have their ear. The truth is that the "I don't care" group is hurting this case as well.

But what about those fringe researchers? You know, the ones who are in this for a profit, monetary or otherwise, so they continue to create outlandish theories and stories to stay relevant. These people give Kennedy researchers a bad name in pop culture because they value their story and beliefs over facts and evidence. My question to them is in the spirit of the McCarthy hearings, "do you have no shame"? But I can answer that question for myself: they don't. It doesn't bother their conscience to lie because they have sold themselves internally that their theories are true. In their eyes we are the brainwashed sheep and they are the ones who really "know" what happened to JFK. But they aren't getting away with it because younger people see them as nutty. I personally have talked to teens and college kids in Dealey Plaza about their thoughts on this case and the feedback I get is that they don't want to be seen as one of the fringe researchers that I'm talking about. But, I don't want to waste to much time of them because they probably won't even read this book. In their eyes I'm an agent of trickery who is a threat to their grandiosity and ballyhoo. The solution to these people is simple: if you don't feed it, it's dies.

And last but certainly not least, there's the younger people who are involved in this case. Make no mistake about it, we are the future. People can argue about the single bullet theory till judgment day, but if we don't keep this case alive then those debates will eventually cease since no one will know what a single bullet is in the first place. I hope you read this book with caution. I hope you understand that we are a blessed generation to take on this case in the year 2018. There have been many patriarchs of this case who have died waiting to see what we have now. I'm talking about men and women who slaved away for years, pouring through documents and holding the government accountable, when you or I hadn't even made our appearance on planet earth.

Let us be humble then. Let us work together despite our disagreements and not make this case our identity. Let us not continue to make the same mistakes the old guard has if we care about JFK and his legacy. We can learn a lot from those who have gone before us, but we cannot destroy one another through gossip and personal attacks if we care to make a change. We have a great opportunity to finally get a resolution about that November day and woe to us if we let it slip away. This case does matter. It's all around us. We must complete the history books. Our future depends on it.

And there are many more groups that I'm sure I'm missing. Nonetheless, I hope the reader has grasped my point. There's certain cancers within the JFK community that must be eradicated if we are going to move forward in this case. This book will be a tool, so you can identity what I and other researchers believe are issues you should avoid while in pursuit of the truth. I will detail those roadblocks in the coming chapters and I will close with a call to action. Half of the battle against our human nature is to be aware of our own sins and shortcomings. How can we move forward if we can't acknowledge them in the first place? I hope this book will remove some our blindness and will shift the power of the research community back to its rightful owner: history.

Chapter 1
SOCIAL MEDIA

While social media has helped this case, it also has created an unfortunate issue: everyone online is now an "expert." What I mean is that the standard people use for defining a credible researcher has dropped drastically since the rise of Facebook. In this environment, if I want to be seen as legit, my road to success is simple. I first must gain some basic knowledge about the case. I then need to hang around long enough to pick up some of the same debating points that others use to back my beliefs when they are challenged. After I get those things down, I need to join a JFK assassination Facebook group and initiate people who I disagree with through my posts. Once some controversy gets started, and I find out that others disagree with me, I will create my own group and become my own authority on this case. Before you know it, boom, I'm certified.

Now, I want to say that there are also some positive things about these groups, and I enjoy a lot of the people that interact online. I'm not saying that we shouldn't have any groups or that we shouldn't engage in debate. What I'm pointing out is how there are certain people who have followed the process

I described above so they could have a pulpit to preach from without being challenged. They do this because they want to make a name for themselves in this case. These are the ones who grow increasingly angry when you disagree with them. They will block you the first chance they get once they figure out you won't bow down to their belief. They dispense ridiculous theories like candy and they only allow those who will eat it to hang around them. How does this help promote the legacy of this case? It doesn't.

Of course, behind our keyboards we don't have to deal with controversy if we don't want to. We can simply erase someone from challenging our worldview if we wish to. That enables us to remain an authority to ourselves. The risk of this behavior is found in the results. When we do this, we become more and more isolated and ignorant because we have ceased to form any other opinions than our own.

And that's why social media has become a major issue for the JFK research community. We have taken history and treated it as a chat group. One man on a Facebook page has no right to berate someone else for civilly challenging their views because he doesn't own this history. That information you're typing out isn't your original thought. You had to learn it from someone else that came before you. You might have some power because you're an administrator on a Facebook page, but that doesn't mean you have the power to control what everyone thinks about this case. Is it not arrogant to assume we know every single thing about every topic involved in the Kennedy assassination? I'm confident that most people wouldn't claim they have it all down, but if you read some of the back and forth in the comment boxes then you would be led to believe that some actually do.

CHAPTER 1

The truth is that once this case has become who we are through an online presence then we can't objectively teach others about it. If that happens we have lost the view that we are ambassadors of history. We aren't supposed to claim we are the lone fountain of all JFK knowledge; we're supposed to be searching for the truth. We can't search for truth when we act as if we've already arrived and we own this information for ourselves.

I often wonder how JFK would have acted online. What would he think if he saw someone claiming they owned the history about his own death? How would he react to all the slander and malice that is created over those who debate his legacy? Isn't it a bit hypocritical to beat the drums of Camelot and claim we are "doing this for our President" while we behave completely contrary to how he called us to act towards one another? We aren't off the hook because we're online. As a matter of fact, the future of the Kennedy assassination IS online. Knowing that, we would do well to examine our own attitudes towards one another and consider how protective we are about our place in this case. What's our motive behind running a group? Why can't we be challenged? Why do we act as if we own history? Why do we act contradictory to the values of the man that we claim we are fighting for?

Most importantly, social media can allow us to not see someone else as a human being if we aren't careful. As I stated above, it's easy to get online and argue with someone about the facts of this case and then demonize them if we don't agree with their theory. We need to be careful not to go there because it doesn't do anything except create drama for the JFK research community. To do something over and over again and expect a different result is insanity, correct? Then why does the JFK community continue, year after year, to travel down the path of self destruction through online in fighting? What does it profit this case to behave like that?

As a younger researcher, who has experience in educating my peers about this case, the word on the street is people are getting tired of seeing the in online circus. We must pay attention to that judgment. If people aren't attracted to how we are presenting ourselves then they aren't going to hear our message, no matter how important it may be. We could, however, march on in our grandiosity and believe we aren't to blame when it comes to people's disinterest in this case, but that also isn't moving anything forward because it isn't the truth. All of us should take that old wisdom to heart when we are online discussing this case, "a soft answer turns away wrath." I plead with the JFK community to please practice that today. We cannot afford to continue to destroy one another online.

"A fool takes no pleasure in understanding, but only in expressing his opinion."

Proverbs 18:2

Chapter 2

Gossip and Slander

This is a painful reality in the research community. I've met a lot of quality researchers who have wanted to help in this case, only to see them crumble into a disillusioned victim because of the jealousy and slander that so often plagues us. Not everyone is like this. I also know a lot of researchers who are genuine at heart. However, if we're honest, there are those who aren't in this with a pure motive. Just ask yourself; What in the world does the gossip and slander of other researchers do to help solve the murder of President Kennedy?

Answer: absolutely nothing. So why do so many people think it's necessary to destroy someone else who they disagree with if doesn't help the case? I think that perspective reveals more about their character than it does about the person they are slandering. Even if what they were saying about their opponent were true, and most of the time it isn't, it still wouldn't help us grow in our knowledge about the case once their flaws were exposed.

That's not say that false teachers shouldn't be exposed for who they are because they should be. As I said in my introduction, there are a lot of fringe researchers who do more harm to the credibility of this community than good. I think those people should be identified and exposed through factual data about their work and character. However, there's a difference between doing that and going on and on with a heart of vindictive slander.

If we've already pointed out what's wrong with a researcher's information, or we've already warned others about their character, there's no point in continuing to beat a dead horse. We love to gossip about another researcher when we hear about personal struggles in their lives because it feeds the resentment that has created the need to slander in the first place. I stay far away from researchers whose hearts are full of resentment and I suggest others do the same. Besides, if they are willing to gossip about others and their work, what makes you believe they won't also be willing to slander you?

Chapter 3
Lies

As hard as it seems to believe, certain researchers will lie about the facts of this case. They do this because there is something deep inside them that desperately wants their theories to be accepted as true. To accomplish this, they must apply certain tactics to sell their beliefs.

One of them is to take things out of context. For example, they will take a statement of an eyewitness and present it to you as the only thing this witness said in their entire testimony. Meanwhile, the researcher knows this is false. They refuse to acknowledge the entire context because if they do it will destroy their theory. Sadly, I fell for this plot time and time again as a younger researcher. I recall being excited when I would read a quote from a certain person about this case, because I thought it finally proved a conspiracy. Later, depressingly, I would find out that the quote was taken out of context and twisted to mean something it wasn't intended to mean. Watch out for false context and faulty quotes while researching the Kennedy assassination. There's more of them out there than you can fathom.

Another tactic they employ is denial, denial, and denial. If you stump a false researcher with the facts they will deny the facts you used to do it and then they will claim you're apart of the conspiracy to kill President Kennedy as well. They don't mind saying such outlandish things because they know no one will hold them accountable for their accusation. I think that people who do this are intellectually lazy as well dishonest about their motives in researching this case.

If someone disagrees with me about the facts, then I don't claim they are an agent of the government. You want to know why? Because I don't have any evidence for that outside of my own opinion. Thus, to brand someone as a part of the conspiracy to kill the President because they schooled you in a debate only means you are hurting this case more than helping it. If you can't admit where you're wrong in your research, then you don't need to be involved in historical study in the first place. Honesty is always the best policy when it comes to research, so we must be careful to not put our bias above where the evidence takes us. If do that we will be okay.

Besides, what are people so afraid of? Why do people seem to be so weary of putting their facts on the table and debating others who disagree with them? I mean, if we really are searching for the truth then wouldn't we want to see if our beliefs can have holes shot through them? When people tell me that they "just don't want to waste their time hearing the other side of what researchers have to say" I think they are gravely mistaken in that approach. That mindset shows a failure to understand the most important part of this case: passing it on to a younger generation and communicating in their language. We can argue the single bullet theory all day long, but if we don't reach out to younger people and mentor them them all that knowledge will be in vain when it passes away.

CHAPTER 3

What does this have to do with honesty? Well, the newer generation of researchers wants to hear both sides of the debate and they don't want to be spoon fed information by people who only present their belief as the gospel. That's just the way it is, and if the research community doesn't realize that then they will become more outdated than they already are. I'm sure that's hard to hear, but for the sake of preserving their work, it's the truth that must be swallowed. It's simply not intellectually honest to only give people one side of a historical study. You must allow people to develop their own critical thinking. It will work out in the long run because people will trust us more knowing that we have them the freedom to choose based on the evidence before them.

Of course, there are those who have allowed this case to become their possession, and they would hate for that to be stripped away, or to be replaced by someone younger. Because of that, I do realize that those people will never pass any information on to anyone. That's for another discussion though.

My point in this is that dishonesty in this case has many different shades and colors but they all are destroying the community from within. If we lie about our research, or we refuse to see where we're wrong, or we write others off because they don't say what we want to hear, we're only hurting the legacy of President Kennedy, and the legacy of the great researchers who have gone before us. It's simply dishonest do practice any of those things in our research and then claim we know the truth about this case.

Chapter 4
STATESMANSHIP

JFK was arguably the greatest statesman to ever grace the White House. Yes, his character was flawed in certain areas, but he usually showed class—even towards his harshest enemies. I hope we can strive to be a statesman in our research as well. As JFK told us in his American University Speech—we are all mortals; we all breathe the same air. In the spirit of that speech, I also hope we can treat one another with class and respect.

One of the most disappointing times in my research experience was when I witnessed how ugly some people could get in their search for the truth. I'm not naive or thin skinned anymore about this. It's a reality that I accept. But I also know it's a travesty of justice against JFK.

It seems to be a strange contradiction, doesn't it? As I stated earlier in this book, we tend to admire JFK to the point of becoming defensive about his legacy. Yet, we also can fail to follow his example while defending his legacy. One moment we're mad that the government has hid things and lied to us, yet some will turn around and hide evidence from other researchers inside their own house. Others will simply lie about another researcher in order to get ahead.

CHAPTER 4

This is the travesty I'm writing about. Do we not realize that the world is watching when we act so hypocritically towards one another? How long can we continue to ignore the fact that we are hurting JFK's legacy by not acting as he did while claiming that we admire his convictions?

There are many quality researchers in this case, who hold all different types of beliefs. I don't mean for it to sound like this applies to them because it doesn't. I'm speaking about the ones who are offended right now by reading this. Why are you offended? I surely hope it's not because I called us to carry on the spirit of the new frontier by practicing statesmanship. I also hope it's not because I'm speaking the truth and that has provoked some prideful feelings inside you.

I don't get any pleasure out of that. It doesn't build me up to tear others down. What builds me up is to see things grow and reach their full potential. Thus, you can be offended at me, but please look in the mirror and consider what I'm saying before you write me off. What would happen if we made it our goal in the next year to act like a statesman online, and in person, while we're debating this case? What if we decided we were going to be the ones who wanted to restore the majestic overtones of the days of JFK by approaching others with class. Are we willing to take such a challenging self evaluation? I hope so.

But, how do we do this? What are some practical ideas for us to reform? Let's start by going back and reading some of our messages and comments to others throughout the last year. Let's see how we matched up to JFK in regard to statesmanship. Are we embarrassed at how we acted? Are we hurting this case through those actions? Are we blind to it? Are we driving others towards the truth or away from it?

It's okay to feel convicted about it. If the truth is told...I'm guilty as well. But, today is a new day and no one can control how I react to things but me. If I'm provoked by an upset researcher, let follow my own advice and be a statesman in the example of our late President...John F. Kennedy. If I do this, then I'm an asset to this case rather than a liability.

Chapter 5
A Lack of Younger Students

I don't want to be harsh on this point, nor do I want to be viewed as unrealistic. I realize it's not easy to get my generation involved in much of anything. We are the "I don't care" generation. We know more about our I Phones than we do about the current events going on around us.

However, I hope the older researchers realize that their work will need to be passed on to younger minds for it to survive. This means it's a top priority for us to reach out to younger people about the importance of JFK's assassination... no matter how difficult it may be. I'm not saying we have to raise up an army of researchers. Even if we're able to reach one, that's better than none. In any case, this is crucial to the overall future of this case.

Let me be respectful in my approach to this. I want to say that I'm a younger man who looks up to my elder researchers. I never want to seem arrogant in my worldview towards you guys. You, and many before you, have sacrificed a lot for the sake of this case, and you also have revealed many pieces of information that have been vital to getting us closer to solving this mystery. If it weren't for you, there wouldn't be a me.

What I'm trying to sell to you guys is that your legacy, and the legacy of this case, all depends on the development of younger researchers. Please hear me out for a minute on that thought.

When I was reaching out to veteran researchers for my first book, I received positive and negative feedback. There were a lot of people who helped me as much as they could, and there were those who didn't. I was surprised by those who responded negatively because I had assumed that any older researcher would be excited to share their information with me. While it was discouraging at times, I'm not mad at them. I understand their reluctance. However, I decided I would press forward without their blessing and prepare to challenge their perspective on why it was important to respond positively when I came to them for information.

It isn't important because I'm going to tell them something that they haven't heard before. It's important because how you treat me affects how hungry I become for the same research you're committed too. One of the reasons why the movie "JFK" ignited so many people to start caring about this murder again was because it didn't disqualify anyone from their own personal journey. Are we like that? Do we help people press on in their journey or do we cleverly manipulate them to quit? Do we encourage others to search like we search, or have we become the old grumpy men and women who sit on the front porch and complain about how those darn kids don't do things the way we used to?

As I said earlier, I know we aren't an easy group to reach, but that's not an excuse to not try. In October of this year the remaining JFK files will be released in full, unless President Trump says otherwise. You guys (and ladies) have worked many years to see this day, and you deserve all the credit for getting them released in the first place. What I beg of you, as a younger researcher, is not to stop once you read them. Reach out to us. Train us. Share your passions and convictions. Don't quit when you can't reach one. Reach out to another. Eventually we will catch on if you are contagious and fair.

If you do this, you will be a great servant regarding moving this case forward. You will have created another researcher to carry the torch. Ask not what the JFK case can do for you, ask what you can do for the JFK case.

Chapter 6
The Fringe Researchers

Since it's earliest days, this case has been plagued by fringe researchers. These people have done more damage to the reputation of sound researchers than any "disinformation" campaign that the government could ever conjure up. Modern pop culture giggles and blushes at the thought of the Kennedy assassination...all thanks to the the silly theories and outlandish behavior that these type of "researchers" have peddled throughout the last half century.

But, even worse, they don't care. They have sold themselves that they are the ones who are telling the truth and all of us are nuts or mislead. This is why I want to alert the research community that they have handled these people in the wrong fashion. I've seen some quality researchers compromise their morals to team with them, and I've also seen others stoop to their level to expose them. Neither one of those approaches will work to eradicate or discredit them in the long run.

It's important to understand that these people have no standards for truth, so trying to debate the facts with them is a waste of time. You are at risk of strengthening them when you do this because it gives them a martyr complex. They take

CHAPTER 6

your apologetics and then turn them on you by claiming they are being persecuted for the "truth." Therefore, don't engage them head on. Write blogs about the falsehoods they preach. Do podcasts. Write books on them. Flood the internet with information and warnings about the wolves in researchers clothing. But no matter what you do, please stop challenging them head on. That will only mix your name into theirs and who wants that?

Please don't compromise either. We must have some dignity in our work and stand up for the truth we claim to believe. (Standing up means doing what I said above and not inviting them into your camp to smooth things over and find a middle ground for the sake of peace. This will only give them a stage to further promote their falsehoods). Stop having them at your events to speak and stop promoting their work. Stop giving them a podium to spread their propaganda. Stop encouraging them in their lies.

It's 2018. That means it's crucial to this case to not let these people get their hands on the new information that's about to flow out. Once they have it they will destroy it from within your camp if you are too passive to stop them. Please don't allow yourself to research this case for this many years, only to fail all of us in the last days because you wavered in your commitment to holding others accountable for what they say about our President's death.

Now, I do think we should be compassionate towards these people's followers because a lot of the time they just don't understand who it is that they are following. The fringe generals tend to use exciting conspiracy trickery to deceive the uneducated into believing their lies.

Thus, how we act towards them will matter as much as

what we tell them we know. We surely won't get anywhere by mocking them.

Stay clear. Don't engage. Point out their bad research and bad character if you can prove it. Don't compromise. Don't get personal. Protect this case.

Chapter 7
Lone Assassin

The lone assassin researchers are usually in the minority when it comes to this case. While a lot of others assume that this makes their opinion irrelevant, I believe that's the lazy way of countering their research. What I mean is that just because most of the country believes something opposite to what they believe doesn't mean they're wrong. Therefore, it would be wise to talk to them and ask them how they came to their conclusions before we use the mob's vote to prove they are wrong.

Of course, if I'm honest, this isn't always an easy task for those who believe in a conspiracy. The lone assassin community has the reputation for being snarky, if not condescending, in their debate style. You talk to some of them and wonder if they really want you to know the truth or if they just want to be right, so their ego feels better. I think it's a little of both, depending on who you're talking with about this case.

I have many lone assassin friends and I don't mean to offend them, but what I've said above is the truth of how their sub group is seen. I hope to point it out so there is a checking of the conscience regarding how we treat those who challenge us.

The old saying is true that someone doesn't remember what you said as much as they remember how you said it.

I will also say that lone assassin researchers aren't treated very well by those who hold to different views about President Kennedy's murder. I have personally witnessed the malice spewing from the keyboards of conspiracy believers before these researchers can even complete a sentence. This shouldn't be the case.

Does the JFK community really want to complete history with the idea that you can't learn anything from a lone assassin researcher? To my conspiracy friends: what are you afraid of? Are you afraid they might poke holes in your beliefs if you interact with them? (I've talked to some of the top lone assassin researchers in the world and they didn't change my views about everything, but they did clear a lot of trash away for me.).

In a strange way, the lone assassin researchers are exactly what this case needs. They are the guard dogs against JFK heresy. If we are honest with ourselves, we will admit they have debunked a lot of silly theories over the years by sticking to certain provable facts in their research. Why does the conspiracy branch hate to admit that? Is it pride? Is it because they were snarky towards us? Is it because we hold a grudge against anyone who doesn't view the world the same way we do?

We cannot claim they are close minded if we are guilty of not hearing them out. We can't claim they are unteachable if we refuse to learn from them. We can't claim they are unfriendly if we haven't made an effort for friendship. Like it or not, they are your fellow researchers. The lone assassin community and the conspiracy community are tied together inside the history of this case.

It's time we started acknowledging that. It's time we started to bridge the gap for the sake of history. Treat others how you want to be treated.

Chapter 8
Conspiracy Researchers

These researchers are in the majority when it comes to this case. Most of the books, documentaries, and other fanfare circle around the belief that President Kennedy was killed as a result of a conspiracy. This is why we must be careful to not leverage that support in an effort to hush everyone who isn't in agreement with us.

We can't rely on what the masses say and claim that's proof that there was a conspiracy. The 2017 Presidential election was just another example that polls are often unreliable or bias in their foundation. Thus, I wouldn't want my friends in the research community to stop relying on evidence because we're leaning on the comfort of familiarity.

The other issue with this group is that they often become overcome with emotion while debating this case. I'll admit that's easy to do. We are trying to prove a conspiracy when there isn't a lot of hard, prove it in court, evidence behind and that often leads to a frustrating road of research. We can't take that frustration out on others. We simply must keep pressing for those tiny pieces of the puzzle that we need, not relying on emotion, but instead focusing in on the grey areas of this case.

CHAPTER 8

When I did my last book, I challenged Mr. Posner and others on the Silvia Odio incident. I did this because I wanted to see what they would say about it and their opinion didn't change my beliefs. (I still think it's suspicious and can't be written off by saying she's mistaken or mentally ill.). I never lost my cool with those guys, nor did I claim they were wrong because everyone thought they were wrong. Rather, I heard them out and chose to respectfully disagree.

This is what the conspiracy researchers should encourage one another to do. We shouldn't rely on polls and emotions as much as we should rely on civil discourse and stronger evidence. It won't hurt anyone to debate these guys. I promise they don't all work for the CIA.

Lastly, the conspiracy researchers tend to be compromising as of late. I say this because I've seen people throwing out all their morals to side with anyone who will believe in a conspiracy alongside them. This is a destructive pattern that's developing within our community and I hope it bothers others as much as it bothers me.

Please be aware of who you are letting inside your walls. You never know what the consequences might be long after you're gone. I would rather be alone in my beliefs than to stand with those who have perverted the facts of this case for their own selfish ambition and quick cash. We're better than that, and there's plenty of grey areas we can focus in on without having to buddy up with charlatans to validate our opinions.

Chapter 9
Thoughts on the Afterlife

What drives your worldview? What are your beliefs and where did they originate? These are questions that most of us answer to flippantly. Yet, we cannot escape the reality that all of us have a belief system that originated somewhere. Subjectivism cannot change that fact, no matter how cleverly it's cloaked behind intellectualism or emotion. Which brings me to my point: out beliefs are what drives our worldview and that should scare us unless we are confident in where we come from or where we are going.

You see, I grew up in a southern town that sold people a little religion mixed in with a lot of day room slogans. "Trust in Jesus and you will be forgiven" is what I was taught. However, that didn't make any sense to me because my beliefs and worldview weren't shaped inside church walls as a child. I was a heartless unbeliever and proud of it. So, when people tried to tell me that I needed Christ to save me, it didn't compute with me because it never shook my foundational worldview. Why should I believe in Christ? Who is that? Why do I need to be forgiven? It all seemed like a silly story to me until I ran out of time in life due to an ever-increasing drug addiction.

CHAPTER 9

That addiction eventually led me to a Pastor in Texas who would forever reshape my outlook on life. This man was intelligent and educated. He wasn't just a dry intellectual either. He spoke with weight and conviction. He challenged my belief system and rocked me to my core. I never really took the time to ponder my beliefs because I had never been challenged to do so. After a few meetings with the Pastor, the "believe in Jesus for salvation" was no longer just a southern tradition. It now pricked the most undesirable parts of my will. I was lost and needed a Savior, not because I did bad things or needed a better life, but because my sin against God and my love for myself was killing me.

I no longer had time for a cheap lesson about God's grace or an angry rant from a neighborhood atheist. I was quickly fading, and my worldview had failed me. Thus, my mentor and friend asked me to allow him to challenge my views and that was the moment I finally came to conclusion that I didn't know where my beliefs had originated from. Christ and His Word filled that void over a period of time through studies and mentorship. He opened my eyes to my sin and He then showed me what He had done for me on the cross. He died for my sin and his death caused me to forsake my old life and trust in Him alone to build me a new one.

And indeed, He did. After years of biblical study and character building I became a man who knew where he stood. I now know my foundation. I know why I'm a Christian. My worldview and belief system can be accounted for through God's Word and all the Wisdom that is found inside it. This process has brought me great peace in an ever-turbulent world where people are scrambling to define who they are and why their voice matters.

I'm thankful for my Pastor because he loved me enough to challenge my beliefs. It was the wounds of this friend that changed my life forever. So, since part of this book was about the differing beliefs of the JFK research community, I wanted to return the favor to you and ask: why do you believe what you believe about life and the afterlife, and where do those beliefs originate from?

Chapter 10
Reach out to a Younger Person

I respect the JFK research community because they represent what a democracy should be about. They have fought for years, even amid what I believe is unfounded criticism and mockery, to hold the government accountable for their secrecy about the assassination. I have also had the privilege to work with many of my heroes when it comes to the JFK assassination research community. Most of them are tremendous people who are climbing a steep hill against opposition. I have much more to learn from them as time rolls forward, but I do think they err on one point: there isn't an urgency to reach out to younger people about this case.

Because of that I reached out to many of them throughout the last three years. I have been opposed and accepted, but I have yet to be asked "how" we can move forward in educating younger minds about this case. I don't find much pleasure in being heard if people don't want to move into action. I fear many in this case rest when they do have a voice, but I'm not satisfied with that. We must execute a plan to get our youth convicted about history or our work may be in danger of collecting dust in the Baylor library.

I think the process of educating younger people begins with forming genuine relationships with them. This mean we should invite them to our conferences, events, and book signings. I often take my young friends with me when I go to Dealey Plaza, so they can soak in the experience of the being there, rather than just hearing me ramble on about the Warren Report over dinner. It sometimes sparks an interest in them and then we discuss the case on the way home. It really is that simple.

Why in the world would the community not want to do that? Why wouldn't they want to share as much as they could with younger researchers, so this case could be kept alive? Are we sometimes eager to get rid of younger people because we see them as an irritant, or just another individual writing a JFK book for money? I can't say that I know all the motives, but I will say that judgement was incorrect when it came to my interest. I wasn't just another guy writing a conspiracy book with regurgitated information that I had stole from a blog. I was a passionate researcher who wanted to let the research community know that I cared about this case and wanted to promote it at all costs.

In all honesty, while I still respect most of the community, they are missing out on a great opportunity to expand this case beyond their lifetime. This case isn't just boring history. It's special. That's why people come from all over the world to the plaza just to see the X in the street. It means something to people to know there is a mystery behind the murder of their late President. Because of that, you don't have to sell the content, as much as you need to show good character while teaching it to others. So, please let us all put our words into action. Reach out. Sacrifice some of your free time and don't

CHAPTER 10

be an elitist. JFK believed in getting the youth of America involved in service and politics, so we can follow his beliefs accordingly. Besides that, these younger students may be the ones who carry your work to completion long after you're gone. It's easy to blow us off now, but one day this country might need us, and we will only go as far as you're willing to lead us.

Chapter 11
PERSONAL THOUGHTS FROM RESEARCHERS

"I can make a couple of general points about the state of the community: There have always been *issues*, but they certainly do seem to be a bigger factor these days.

"My gut feeling is that the public JFK debate now looks a lot like the public debates about just about everything else, which is not good. That was not the case fifty years ago, I think. That is, JFK-specific matters are not the driving force behind the growth of internal issues.

"Perhaps there are some topics on which civil public debate is possible on the web—such as Bach's keyboard tuning systems—maybe.

I expect that you know a lot about how a community with a controversial common interest works (or fails) from your experience with the drug treatment and counseling community.

"One relevant factor in the JFK community is that nobody has any authority to tell anyone else what to do, or what to focus on. With a few exceptions, researchers are not dependent on institutional or financial support from anyone else.

"Thanks to the internet, people don't have to rely on other

community members for validation—it's easy to find supporters among the under-informed."

Paul Hoch, Researcher

"I'm sometimes attacked and called names simply because I don't share the popular belief. If I respond in kind, the discussion will cease. I'd rather the information flow continue so I try to forge ahead in civil discourse as best I can. I know there's sometimes a silent observer. My civility is for them. Particularly if they're young.

"The Kennedy assassination is a very contentious subject, but cordial exchange is possible. Attacking each other might discourage some young enthusiasts away from this important history. Let's show them we can come together and discuss the history of John Kennedy in the respect he deserves. We can do this even if we don't agree."

Fred James, Lone Assassin Researcher

"The internet is the best and worst of inventions: it is a wonderful tool to advertise your wares and research, yet, at the same time, anyone can claim to be a *researcher* and expound upon silly notions (blobs in photos allegedly being gunmen; the old man-in-the-doorway stuff; etc.). A lot of squabbling and in-fighting, but, again, a lot of great people. Researchers get mad if you side with one or the other or just attend one or the other's conference(s)!

"Some great books coming up; JFK's 100th birthday; the CIA files—interest will never die in the Kennedys (look at the *Jackie* movie, for example) or the assassination—JFK is still our last assassinated president, millions still remember him, and millions more view images (still and motion; YouTube, etc.) of his attractive self and his beautiful wife and kids—and sadly, his horrible death. Triumph and tragedy—the Kennedys have it all."

Vince Palamara, Conspiracy Researcher and Author

"The JFK Community is typical of any very large group of people from different walks of life who share an interest. We are filled with fringe people on all sides. We are full of disinformationists and snitches and people who just want to feel important by inserting themselves in such a horrific and notable event in history. We are also full of passionate, honorable, patriotic people who want to find the truth and know that our government lied to us.

"What we should do is get to know each other one on one. Know who we trust, know who we don't. We need to think critically. We need to study personal, political and financial agendas. We need to note how stories do or do not change over the years, and when we become aware of those changes, ask for answers. In other words, we need to do what the CIA, FBI, Secret Service and Police have done for years: know the people in the community.

"Just like any group who is adamant about seeking justice for a blatant injustice, we will have issues. The key is not to *be* an issue, but to *resolve* the issues we can in a civil way."

Gayle Nix Jackson, Researcher and Author

"A majority of my time among the JFK research community

has been a pleasure where I have made great friends, had the opportunity to discuss the case files with experts, and learned from the evidence offered by prior and contemporary scholars. This has provided me a chance to offer some new evidence to answer some of the many questions that remain and reveal popular myths. Some conspiracy critics and advocates have endless personal animosity for each other and dismiss reasonable ideas because they do not fit their predetermined speculations and inherent dislike of those who disagree.

"Often the arguments and hatreds of past decades and current ones serve no purpose but to feed the egos of those conducting them. Enduring grudges will never feasibly end because often neither party can accept being wrong and they seemingly value their ideas and claims over verifiable ones. Indeed, at times, everyone can be wrong, and the mark of a credible investigation is a willingness to admit it and correct the mistake. To ignore this and seek to attack those discovering errors is yet another error.

"Additionally, we must deal with myth-makers, those who rely on popular stories and have claimed for years to have the "final" answers without substantial evidence. Facts do not support them so emotional pleas, innuendo, and seeking to silence detractors are their usual methods. All while a myth-maker's supporter cannot fathom they have been misled and refuse to accept evidence if it contends their chosen beliefs. Yet even these most unreasonable people have taught me something of value. Some will ever refuse to accept verifiable facts, but we shall continue to make progress with or without them.

"Many will advance the case with evidence and reason and others will seek to delay our progress while attempting to force their bad ideas into the public. We must forever resist the easy answers without evidence and seek the difficult ones that require an unbiased inspection and using the context of facts we already possess. Since neither conspiracy advocates nor conspiracy critics yet have the definitive evidence, I regard ideas using verifiable evidence more important than a predisposition for the currently unproven."

Carmine Savastano, Author and Researcher

"As a student of the assassination for the last thirty years I believe we are desperately in need of a new generation of researchers grounded in the ethics of true research and hypothesis testing. The research community has been flooded with snake oil salesman, cherry picking what they need to make their case while ignoring contradictory evidence. With the release of new documents our press taking the documents looking for the headlines, verses the truth creating more myths and inaccuracies. We are absent people who understand what they are looking at when it comes to the evidence.

"A new generation of researchers willing to move beyond the quagmire of YouTube and blogs promoting inaccuracies is essential to our cause. We need a new generation of researchers, committed to let the evidence lead them, willing to let their personal hypotheses be obliterated or proven by the primary source evidence.

"Hypotheses should be tested and learned from by researchers committed the process, for even a disproved hypothesis helps move us forward. This quest for the truth is dependent on people willing to put the truth ahead of their own personal beliefs and theories. History deserves researchers that possess research standards, so that this case, currently bogged down in myths built on a quicksand of misinformation over the last fifty years, can move forward towards reaching an accurate conclusion about the death of President Kennedy grounded in solid fact."

Matthew Scheufele, Researcher

"Who are they? The high-frequency posters on internet discussion groups have no desire to improve. Ensconced in their comfy cocoons, their playpens of arguing, these *researchers* want only to perpetuate their pointless, endless disputes. The Arguers' worst fear is that this case gets solved.

"No, the true researchers don't post, don't argue, don't need an internet presence. They quietly unearth neglected, misunderstood or forgotten clues. They analyze and re-analyze, unafraid to change their minds. With years of hands-on experience in disciplines essential for solving these mysteries, they see theorizing as unnecessary. For the Solvers, the only way to improve is to crack the case."

Ed Bauer, Author and Researcher

"It was said to me when I was starting out that in your generation lies the answers. This is still true I believe, because the younger generation will have all the answers, it is up to you to put the final piece of the puzzle together. We, the 1st, 2nd, and even 3rd generation researchers have laid the ground work and completed 95 percent of the puzzle. You will have access to all the documents that have been withheld, witnesses who came forward recently, and you will have the knowledge passed on from those of us who have come before you.

"Do not be afraid to question everything, but be prepared to have everything questioned. If you want to truly solve this case, go outside Dealey Plaza and work backwards. Open your ears, become a sponge and listen to those older researchers in doing so you will avoid the same pitfalls and disappointments that have come before you.

"Any chance you get to talk to a witness take it, there aren't many left and one day they will all be gone."

*Chris Gallop, Longtime researcher
and founder of JFK: The Continuing Inquiry*

Chapter 12
The Challenge

As many of you know, I'm a researcher who is all about presenting people with both sides of the story. I don't believe you can adequately come to a conclusion in this case unless you are willing to learn about all the different types of theories and conclusions that others have created through time. Since the information surrounding the Kennedy assassination is so massive, we need to hear from others and then test what we heard against the evidence and historical record. One of the easiest ways to break that information down is through a debate style setting. I say this because it enables students to see what holes can be poked in each belief, while it also provides them the ability to see the other side attempt to explain its weaknesses. This is why I'm putting the following challenge in this book.

The list you will read on the next page is called "Having It Both Ways." It was created by lone assassin researchers FJ James, David Reitsez, Jim Hess, and Scott Maudsley; and it was originally posted on the Facebook group "Fair Play For JFK." It attempts to point out certain contradictions in the conspiracy researchers view about this case. It claims that they ignore certain evidence to make a conspiracy fit into the timeline of the assassination. I found it clever and challenging to my belief, and if you're honest with yourself, I think you will as well.

I want to issue a challenge to my fellow conspiracy believers to write a response to this list and email it to me at Jacobmarkuscarter@gmail.com. I will take your response and gladly submit it on my website for everyone to see. (I attempted to have this done before this book came out, but I couldn't get any takers.). I think this will be a huge addition to our understanding of this case and I can't wait to see where it can take us.

Are you ready to meet the challenge?

Having It Both Ways

By FJ James, with Jim Hess, David Reitzes, and Scott Maudsley.

1. Lee Harvey Oswald was an active intelligence operative,
   but has never held an active operator's license.

2. Oswald could not have achieved the shots due to adrenaline, and stress,
   but was cool and collected when Baker pointed a gun at his chest.

3. Ed Hoffman could clearly see the shooters from 200 yards.
   Howard Brennan could not see Oswald from 80 feet.

4. There's no way Oswald could hit a moving target.
   The limousine came to a complete stop.

5. The rifle was well lubricated and should have left oil on the brown paper.
   The rifle was rusted and could not have been fired.

6. Oswald slipped into the movie theater between 1, and 1:07 pm,
   but was at the bus stop at Zang and Beckley at 1:04

7. Marguerite testified Lee was left handed.
   The scope was left mounted and therefore could not have been fired by a right-handed Oswald.

8. The Zapruder film is a hoax which shows evidence of a conspiracy.

The Zapruder film is genuine and shows evidence of a conspiracy.

9. There's no evidence Oswald practiced with the rifle.

The shells used to frame Oswald were probably picked up at the range where he practiced.

10. Hellen Markham is mentally challenged, and unreliable, except when she placed the Tippit shooting at 1:10 p.m.

11. No one saw Oswald descend the stairs, therefore he was not there.

No one saw Oswald on the front steps, but he certainly was there.

12. Oswald left the book depository in a Nash Rambler, but found the time to offer his cab to a woman.

13. The Warren Commission has a magic bullet.

Two bullets entered the president's body from the front and back, then vanished, but that's not magic.

14. Oswald is Prayer Man.

Oswald is Lovelady.

15. Oswald was not able to make it to 10th and Patton on time to kill Tippit,

but made it to the Texas Theater (further away) when someone else shot Tippit.

16. The length of Oswald's bag proves he was innocent; he was probably carrying curtain rods.

Frazier was lying; there was no long bag, and Oswald never said a word about curtain rods.

17. Railroad employees could see gun smoke from the knoll 20 feet away.

Railroad employees could not see, hear, or feel the shooter on the triple underpass 2 feet away.

18. Marina is a proven liar, and cannot be trusted,

except when she says Lee is innocent.

19. The HSCA concluded that JFK was killed as a result of a probable conspiracy.

They also said Oswald fired all the shots that hit people, but that part doesn't matter at the present moment.

20. The money and ring left behind have no evidentiary value,

except when its alleged it was supplied by Ruth Paine to implicate Oswald.

21. The brown paper package didn't have enough wrinkles.

The wrinkles on the brown paper were in the wrong place.

22. The two bullets which hit Kennedy in the front, and back worked their way back out of the wounds,

but it's impossible the bullet in Connally's leg could have done such a thing.

23. Witnesses with information pointing to conspiracy were ignored and never called to testify,

but somehow witnesses were allowed to say they heard more than 4 shots and saw smoke on the knoll.

24. Secret Service agents are criticized for not swarming on the limo to protect JFK,

Agent Greer is criticized for slowing the limousine.

25. Some conspiracists believe those who advocate a lone gunman are actually CIA disinformation agents,

but they know the inner workings of the CIA better than the agents they argue with.

26. We know one or more shots came from the north knoll, because witnesses said so.

One or more shots came from the south knoll, even though not a single, solitary witness said so.

27. The Dallas Police are criticized for not sealing off the building immediately (reacting slow),

but criticized again for identifying the suspect in 40 minutes (reacting fast).

28. Oswald was a highly trained CIA operative,

but needed a bus ride home to change trousers.

29. Oswald has the darkest, and potentially the most damaging secret in American history. He must be silenced,

but first let him finish his press statement on live TV.

30. The government's investigation was the sloppiest, and most poorly conducted investigation in history.

The assassination was the government's most cleverly orchestrated overthrow, and cover-up in history.

Chapter 13
WESLEY BUELL FRAZIER

Around two years ago I was fortunate enough to meet the man who drove Lee Harvey Oswald to work the day he allegedly assassinated President Kennedy. He was classy, and he carried a comforting presence about himself. What I was impressed with was how he calmly answered everyone's questions when it was his time to speak. I was thrilled to hear what he had to say because here was a fellow that had personally experienced Oswald as his friend and coworker. He also was a firsthand eyewitness to the events surrounding November 22, 1963. Others, however, weren't so overwhelmed with his credentials.

As I sat back in the conference room I watched a man, who claims to be a JFK researcher, commit an erroneous mistake while he was questioning Mr. Frazier. You see, Mr. Frazier had stated that Oswald wasn't around him during the assassination and that testimony contradicted what this researcher believed to be true. You would think that no one would dare challenge the account of Mr. Frazier, since, logically speaking, he was there that day. But this man did.

He even dared to raise his voice and argue with the man

who had personally took Oswald to the Book Depository on the morning of the crime.

This was a shameful thing for me to witness as a younger researcher. What arrogance does it take to rebuke someone who actually lived what we strive to study? Even worse, how tragic is it that he put Mr. Frazier through that? Yet, it's sadly becoming a common event for some to indulge in.

I've sat back and watched how some of the witnesses have been treated and it's hard to swallow. I hope that we can rise above such madness and see the foolishness of trying to push our theories down the throats of those who lived it.

We should never become so invested in a certain theory that we grow irate when someone disagrees with us. We certainly shouldn't act that frustration out towards a witness. But that's kind of where we're at now isn't it? Aren't some researchers becoming more and more unrealistic as time passes by? Doesn't it seem like they have wrapped themselves in this case to the point that they can't enjoy anything else in life? I think so, and I also think we should be careful not to fall into the same trap.

There are some researches who have written great books and made many fascinating discoveries along the way. They are praised for their contributions, as they should be, but I cannot side with those who have left their families for this case, or who don't mind exploding on others in anger over a historical topic. That seems a little off if you ask me.

In the final analysis, I hope my story above teaches us a lesson on respect and knowing where we are at. There's a time and place for everything and that was the time and place, but the fellow didn't have the temperament to handle hearing that he was wrong about his theory. I would hope he apologized later to Mr. Frazier afterwards, but I'm not sure. (If he did, I commend him for that.). I also hope we haven't become so entrenched in this case that we neglect those who need us most. By all means, solve the Kennedy assassination, but don't solve it at the cost of losing what's really important in life.

Tony Summers warned me about becoming like that when I did my last book and I'm happy he cared enough to give me such advice. I don't know about you, but I would be horrified to one day learn that the Kennedy assassination was my only legacy. That's why I sometimes take a step away from studying it, so I can pursue other things and refresh my perspective. The case is intoxicating, but it isn't worth the heartbreak of missing out on our present history for the sake of trying to solve our past history. I suppose it all comes down to priorities and how we choose to handle them.

Chapter 14

Interview with JFK assassination witness Mary Ann Moorman Krahmer

Mrs. Krahmer has become somewhat of a friend throughout my JFK lifespan. She is witty, wise, and not afraid to voice her opinion about this case. I cannot imagine how her life has changed since she witnessed the murder of our President over fifty years ago, but I do know she handles herself with class and patience when people calling for information. Because of that I wanted the reader to hear her thoughts about how the research community has affected her life. I think you will enjoy her perspective.

Q. Do you find it funny how a lot of researchers claim they know what happened in Dealey Plaza the day JFK was killed, and they weren't there?

A. No not funny. I find it foolish on their part to say what happened when some weren't even born at that time.

Q. Why do you think they are so off when they claim to be 100 percent correct in their research?

A. I've read that each eye witness can see the very same thing that happened and can have different summaries of what they saw. They can begin with exactly what they see and then as they read other reports of the scene, they can easily begin to think there was more to the story. This then causes a different slant on what they thought they witnesses. As to the researchers as witnesses, they are relying on the actual witness reports, then what they are reading as to what they were told from these witnesses. In the end, so much is being embellished to make it seem more impressive.

Q. That's interesting. As someone who personally witnessed this tragedy, has it been hard for you to see the assassination become such a point of division in our country?

A. Well, I was there mostly to see Jackie as she was a fashion model for me and so elegant. I wasn't into politics at that time and I'm sure I hadn't not voted even at that time. Seeing a president of the United States was certainly out of the ordinary. In the many years that have passed, I have witnessed our government and just how things can be covered up. Even to this day, the country is trying to know the truth of what is really taking place in our world. So, yes, it has been difficult to experience that.

Q. How have the researchers from both sides of the table treated you throughout the years?

A. The researchers have all went out of their way to be extremely pleasant. Over the years, so many have become very dear friends, a few like family. This past year of my life has been beyond the ordinary and several have gone remarkably out of their way to see to me. As you and some of the researchers know, there was one that said I didn't take the picture and he was a little out of the way.

Q. Do you think, in a small way, all of us are tied into the assassination together? (I'm speaking of the researchers from all sides and the witnesses and everyone involved).

A. I do think all are reaching for the final end. The truth of what was the reason for the assassination. I was so in hopes that I would hear the end of the story before I passed on. Don't think it will ever come about as there is too many agencies involved and the truth would be the end of the U.S. It would cause chaos that couldn't be controlled.

Chapter 15
SIMPLE EVIDENCE FOR A CONSPIRACY

The Kennedy assassination is a mystery. Did Lee Harvey Oswald murder President Kennedy alone, or was he encouraged by others to commit the crime of the century? Because of the mass confusion that swirls around this case, I wanted to present a simple guideline of evidence that would prove a possible conspiracy occurred in the death of our late President. However, for us to avoid making this conclusion without credible evidence we must approach the case through logic until discovering A. credible physical evidence, or B. extremely strong circumstantial evidence. It's unquestionable that once we apply these investigative methods we'll see credible physical evidence that Lee Harvey Oswald was an assassin, and strong circumstantial evidence that he didn't act alone.

The following testimonies are eye witness accounts of President Kennedy's assassination. These testimonies are vital to the case because they are given by people who were present at the scene of the crime.

Dallas policeman J.M. Smith, who had been directing traffic on the eastern side of Houston Street, where Elm crosses Houston, testified before the Warren Commission on July

23, 1964. He claimed he didn't know where the shots had originated from, but almost immediately after the shooting a woman came up to him and said "They are shooting the president from the bushes." In response, Patrolmen Smith ran down the street and started checking the area around the grassy knoll. When Smith reached the area behind the picket fence, he said he encountered a secret service agent:

"I felt awfully silly, but after the shot and this woman, I pulled my pistol from my holster and I thought, this is silly, I don't know who I am looking for, and I put it back. Just as I did, he showed me that he was a Secret Service agent...He saw me coming with my pistol and right away he showed me who he was." Smith also stated that the man's "credentials satisfied me and the deputy sheriff." (Seymour Weitzman was the deputy sheriff with Smith; he also told the Warren Commission that he met a fake secret service agent.) Smith even went as far as to say that he sensed "the lingering smell of gunpowder."

Of course, there we're no secret service agents in the grassy knoll area at the time of the assassination, (this has been repeatedly confirmed by the Secret Service itself) so here we find a huge problem for the lone-nut conclusion. If there were no secret service officials on the knoll during or after the shooting, who was this man that Officer Smith encountered, and why was he faking his identity immediately following the shooting?

William Newman, one of the closest eye witnesses to the assassination, testified to Dallas police on Nov. 22, 1963 that he "thought the shot had come from the garden directly behind me that was on elevation where I was...on the curb. I do not recall looking toward the Texas School Book Depository. I looked back in the vicinity of the garden."

CHAPTER 15

S.M. Holland, a railroad supervisor, was near the grassy knoll area when the assassination occurred. He testified that he heard four shots, and that the third shot caused a puff of smoke to appear from the tree line along the picket fence on the grassy knoll. Holland also stated that after the shooting he ran to the picket fence to search for possible evidence of a second gunman. However, when he reached the corner of the fence where he had seen the smoke, a number of policemen were already present. He recalled that there was a station wagon backed up to the fence, and that there was a spot, about three feet by two feet, that looked to him like somebody had been standing there for a long period of time. (It had been raining earlier that day in Dealey Plaza.) Holland stated that there were about a hundred foot tracks on the spot, and there was mud up on the bumper of the station wagon, as if someone had either used it to clean his foot off or stood up on it to look over the fence.

Secret Service Agent Paul E. Landis was riding on the right running board of the follow up car to President Kennedy's limousine. He stated that the third shot came from "somewhere toward the front, right hand side of the road." Landis later told congressional investigators that he was sticking to his story, and that he understood the implications of stating that shots came from two different directions.

Lee E. Bower, a railroad workman stationed in a glass-walled tower about fifty yards north and west of the Book depository, gave the Warren Commission a deposition on April 2, 1964. He said there were several unfamiliar automobiles in the parking lot area in close proximity to the shooting. (This would also put these strange cars near the knoll areas well.) He said he noticed them because he recognized the cars that were parked in the lot regularly, and these cars weren't apart of those regulars. One the unfamiliar cars was a blue and white 1959 Oldsmobile station wagon; another was a 1961 or 1962 Impala. Both were dirty and had out-of-state license plates-(white background with black numbers)-and both had single, white male occupants.

Five years after JFK was killed, Tip O'Neill, former speaker of the house, had dinner with Kenneth O'Donnell and Dave Powers, both of whom had been close friends of President Kennedy, and had ridden in the motorcade with him the day he was assassinated. O'Donnell and Powers recalled to O'Neill that they both had heard shots come from the grassy knoll. O'Neill challenged O'Donnell's account by saying, "That's not what you told the Warren Commission." O'Donnell replied, "Your right. I told the FBI what I had heard, but they said it couldn't have happened that way, and that I must have been imagining things. So I testified the way they wanted me to. I just didn't want to stir up any more pain and trouble for the Kennedy family."

Six witnesses, including three in the motorcade, said they smelled gunpowder around the grassy knoll area. They include Senator Ralph Yarborough, Congressman Ray Roberts, the Dallas Mayor's wife, and two police officers. Seven witnesses on the railroad bridge of the triple underpass said they saw something that appeared to be smoke coming from the grassy knoll.

Almost immediately after the assassination, Dallas Police Chief Jessie Curry radioed to his comrades to "get a man on top of that triple underpass and see what happened up there."

Secret Service Agent Forrest Sorrels, who in charge of the Dallas office, said that he "looked towards the top of the terrace to my right, as the sound of the shots seemed to come from that direction."

CHAPTER 15

In light of these testimonies, it's important to note that the Warren Commission told the American public that there was, "no credible evidence to indicate shots were fired from any place other than the Texas School Book Depository." This quote is even more audacious when you see the statistics of eye witness testimony for yourselves:

There were around 250 people in the plaza that day, 171 of these people gave statements to the Warren Commission in 1964. In short, 76 witnesses said they didn't know where the shots came from; 46 said they came from the book depository; 29 said they came from some place other than the book depository or the grassy knoll; and twenty (surely enough to be counted as worthy of recognition in an official government investigation) said they came from the grassy knoll.

When I spoke with G. Robert Blakey, the former Chief Counsel and Staff Director of the House Select Committee on Assassinations, I was satisfied with the information he made available. Mr. Blakey told me that Lee Oswald's guilt in the murder was undeniable due to strong physical evidence, and the evidence for a shooter from the grassy knoll could be controversial as well. Mr. Blakey attributed his second shooter solution primarily to the testimony of numerous eye witness accounts which he deemed credible. Mr. Blakey still supports the acoustical evidence his experts discovered during the HSCA investigation (1976-1978), but he acknowledges that people have discovered interesting holes in it as well.

In closing, it's the opinion of many that the need of balance in the world is what drives us to desire a deeper meaning to the JFK assassination, but as my good friend Pete Orta points out, "In the times of no conspiracies, only a conspiracy could change the times." In America, the early 1960s were a time of innocence and trust. People didn't think or operate like we do today; they weren't the critics that we tend to be—especially when it came to questioning the government's final accounts on political assassinations. Therefore, my friends quote simply means that if Americans in the '60s weren't the skeptics we are today, then something had to give our culture a reason to be skeptical in the first place (Which comes first; the lie or the doubter?).

The case is still a mystery in some circles. The reason for people's belief in a conspiracy is founded in, as Jefferson Morley calls it, "the circumstances of the crime." The eyewitness testimony of the assassination is more than enough information for any logical person to conclude something sinister may have occurred in Dallas, Texas on November 22, 1963. We in the research field are still waiting for the CIA, the Mexico City Archives, and Cuba to release the remaining files they hold on the JFK assassination, so it shouldn't be seen as outlandish for us to question the Warren report or any other lone nut conclusion.

Chapter 16
PROFILING THE DARKER SIDE OF THE RESEARCH COMMUNITY

As a young author in the JFK research community I have the advantage of looking at this case with a fresh set of eyes. I am also an experienced character profiler (or criminal if you will), and this gives me some insight into other areas of this case that few people seem to touch on. One of the goals of this book, is to help reform the research community for the sake of history. I've been working extremely hard to accomplish that task.

One of the ways to move forward in this process is by exposing the bad character of certain researchers. I do not believe these people can ever be persuaded to honesty, so I will not attempt to contact them personally. Saying that, I want to say this from the get go. I see a lot of quality researchers waste their time by debating these types of people, all in the hope that they can expose them in their true colors. This is a misguided strategy because direct confrontation is never the way to expose a narcissist, sociopath, or psychopath. As a matter of fact, it only furthers their cause.

Simply put, we're wasting our time trying to call these guys out. We need to take a step back and create a better game-plan if we wish to shift the research community into logic. I believe I have that game-plan. I think if we educate other people on what a "wolf in sheeps clothing" looks like, and we ignore their outlandish claims, we will be able to push them off the debate stage for good, simply because there will be very few left to engage them.

So, how do we do this? We should start by profiling *who* the researchers are behind their keyboards and stop focusing on *what* they claim to know. Knowing who someone is will oftentimes tell you a lot about why they claim to know certain things. For example, a researcher may claim to know who was behind the picket fence on November 22, 1963—yet have no evidence to back their theory up-and still stand by their claim no matter what contradicts it. How can they be so blind? Are they lying through their teeth or are they self deceived? What kind of person can take the death of a man and build lies around his case in order to sell a theory? My Answer: Someone who is selfish in their character has no problem with doing any of that. For them, the ends justify the means.

You will never convince these people of their lies because they have sold themselves into an alternative reality. What I'm saying is that some "researchers" have lied to themselves for so many years that they now believe those lies to be truth. This causes these types of people to be very detailed in their stories, and to have the ability to look you straight in the eyes while telling it. (Practice makes perfect.) Over time this process weakens people's discernment. I can't tell you how many times I've seen logical researchers buy into tall tales because, they argue, no one could be that detailed and straight forward if it they weren't telling the truth—could they?

Indeed, liars are great at impression management. This means they are masters at presenting themselves in an image that they know people want to see. But why do they operate like this in the first place? What drives people to participate in such insanity? This is where character profiling can come in handy. For the most part I have noticed that the fakes in this case fall into three different profiles:

1. *Narcissists:* People who are only interested in themselves. These types love to talk about themselves and demean others who dare criticize them or their work. It is useless to debate them, or to try to correct them, because they thrive on attention and are usually charismatic enough to gain a following. If you attack them then you will only enable them to become a martyr for their following. Narcissists thrive on attention, so please stop giving it to them.

2. *Sociopaths:* These types love themselves to the point that they lack empathy for others. They are also master manipulators and liars. They know how to use others' emotions against them to get people to do their bidding. They can cry on the spot or compartmentalize their identity, depending on who they're in front of. This is why certain researchers can sell their false stories to the masses. The use their superficial glib and charisma to deceive and they don't mind doing this because they don't have a conscience in the first place.

Directly confronting a sociopath can be a very dangerous thing to do. You must hold a sociopath to a workable timeline and not get lost in their emotions. Once you refuse to buy into their stories, and you don't allow them to manipulate you with emotions, they will show their real colors if they can't get what they want.

Also, if you are debating a sociopath, never give them

any personal information about yourself. They will use it to their advantage.

3. *Psychopaths:* These types occupy the darker side of the JFK community. They are often the most likable people. They hold down steady jobs and even have the middle-class family to boot. My point is that they look normal to us. They aren't like sociopaths because they don't have emotional outbursts or sloppy plans inside their tool boxes. They are very calculated and difficult to discern. However, they do have a weakness. They believe they are smarter than everyone around them. They have huge egos and they love to boast about their strengths and accomplishments. They also cannot talk about the feelings of others for to long because it frustrates them. They want the topic to be about themselves or their work and nothing else. If you want to know if you are dealing with a psychopath, then simply keep the topic on empathy.

Talk to them about JFK's life or others in the community who are good people. They will soon grow bored with this because they are only stimulated by who or what they can dominate.

If that doesn't work, then challenge their accomplishments or knowledge on a certain topic. They cannot handle such criticism without exposing who they are. They will be offended that you cannot see their "greatness" or "importance" in this case.

Scary isn't it? Yet, it reveals a lot about the research community and why so many irrational people seem to be drawn inside it. The root cause of their attraction is that this case is the perfect breeding ground for their type of character to thrive in. It's a historical case where a lot of the people they make claims about have already passed away. This means they can say what they want about the deceased because they aren't there to defend themselves against their charges. Don't think they aren't aware of that fact. Even worse, they also love the attention they get from their detractors. They use this as a tool to draw more people into their poisonous web. As I previously pointed out, when their theories are attacked they become the victim in their followers' eyes and their popularity grows even bigger. If you want to know if any researcher fits that description, then ask yourself the following questions:

How dishonest are they?

Is this case more about JFK or themselves?

How do they handle criticism?

In closing, I want to say this isn't a shot at anyone in particular. I'm aware that people might be tempted to take this personally, but I'm most likely not talking about you if you think I am. We all have certain traits of the dysfunctional personalities I've described and it's a healthy sign if we can admit that. However, there are some among us who are toxic to the research community. If it offends them so be it. I hope to expose those who practice such sickness and I'm willing to train others to do the same. In that, we hopefully can begin to reform the community in a healthier way.

The goal of this speech, I hope, has been accomplished. I want people to be able to identify who a researcher is, and after they do, I want them to know how to handle them. If we wish to flush out those who seek to use JFK's death as a tool to build their personal kingdoms, then we must know how to identify their inner workings first. Stay safe my friends. Fight for the cause of preserving history from those who seek to steal it.

In Closing

The 2017 JFK files are pouring out and some are still sealed while we await a final answer from President Trump. I'm as excited as anyone to see what's in them. I think we can all agree, lone assassin and conspiracy believers, that it's an amazing time to be alive. We're about to see history unfold before our very eyes. With these files, this case will come more into focus and we will be better equipped to understand the historical context that surrounded the Kennedy assassination.

What I fear, however, is that we are on the brink of becoming so divided that we won't have the unity we need to correctly discern what we're reading. If you are a lone nut advocate, then you already believe the files all point to Oswald's guilt. Likewise, if you are a conspiracy believer then you believe they all will point towards a conspiracy. Since there is hardly any civil communication between the two sides, and even in fighting amongst the two camps, I find it hard to believe that people can lay their preconceived bias down to consider what someone has to say about the files or anything else.

This is the main reason why I wrote this book. I can't stand to see people who have come so far, and researched something for so long, tear one another apart through snarky comments and prideful debates. I assumed that I would catch flak for

IN CLOSING

pointing that out. I knew if I identified the struggles of the research community some would buck back, but it's worth it to me if one person changes their behavior towards another person who disagrees with them.

As I've stated many times before, history does not belong to one particular individual. You can't say you own it and neither can I. It doesn't matter how much I read about this case or who discovers what, we didn't get to 2017 alone and we won't make it out alone. We all need each other to complete what the early JFK researchers started. It's human nature to pursue individualism, but this case is to big for one researcher to claim that they don't need to negotiate with their opposition. How in the world can we expect to correctly understand the context of this case when we only believe what one side believes and we refuse to listen to anything that contradicts it? Do you really believe that one side has every single fact down and the other side has absolutely nothing to offer? I hope not.

In this work I have tried to make a difference that might shift toxic perspectives from inside the research community. In certain ways we are stronger than ever, but in other ways we are also crumbling. The divide is growing. We must decide soon about the topics I've addressed throughout this book. Are we going to continue devouring one another, or are we going to find a middle ground through respect and civility?

JFK's legacy depends on us now. Like it or not, we are the ambassadors for Camelot. When someone thinks of JFK, they also think of the research community. How we act towards one another, and what we claim to know about this case, matters when it comes to how Joe public views the late President Kennedy. Because of that we should all examine ourselves and see where we could do better.

Use the tools in this book if you don't know where to start. That's why I wrote it. I want to make a change for the sake of preserving history. I want us to be healthy. I want a resolution. Please join me in my efforts as we try to avoid the mistakes of the past. The in fighting must cease. We must work together to grab the remaining files. We must treat one another with respect. We must study in the spirit of JFK.

Acknowledgments

I want to thank my mother for her unconditional love and service towards me. I love you mom. Thank you, Mike and Paula Parker, for your hard work as my publishers and friends. You guys are top notch and I love to work with you. I hope I have represented Wordcrafts press well. Thank you, Pastor Pete and Kelli Orta. You guys hold a special place in my heart. I will never be the same because of your undying love and commitment towards me. Thank you, Dorian, Jett, Keen, and Zade. You guys have been such a joy to my life and I can't wait to see where the Lord takes you. Thank you Mauricette Jorgenson for your editing work. Hopefully my words are kinder because of your insight. Thank you to everyone who contributed to this book, and also to the JFK research community. You guys are awesome. I want to give my church, Cottonwood Creek Church, a shout out. I'm thankful for everyone there, as well as the love and support that you have shown me. I want to give all the honor and glory to Jesus my Savior. He truly changed me from the inside out and I can't begin to express how thankful I am for it. I am eternally grateful for my salvation in Christ and for the time I've spent being trained for life at In Triumph.

In loving memory of the late Sherry Fiester: Thank you for your kindness to me when I first poked my head into the

research community. While I'm saddened by your loss, I won't forget the example you set for me. Even my younger friends remember how you embraced us.
   RTR

About the Author

Jacob Carter, born in the great state of Alabama (Roll Tide), is a best-selling Author and the Director of In Triumph, a faith-based ministry that gives younger men a second chance through mentorship.

In 2010, Carter was suffering from a severe drug addiction and facing criminal charges. Through a series of unlikely circumstances, he was connected with the founders of In Triumph, Pete and Kelli Orta.

After a long process of mentorship and biblical studies, Jacob was a new creation. The people who knew him were astonished at how much he had changed in such short period of time. He chose to enter In Triumph's internship program, where trained to work full time in the ministry. After graduating from the program he served as a counselor for a year before before being promoted to the position of Director.

Carter is considered an expert on the Kennedy assassination by the Sixth Floor Museum in Dallas, Texas, and he has written extensively about that topic

Carter is also an avid Alabama Crimson Tide supporter, and his book about the Alabama football program, The RipTide (WordCrafts Press), reached Number 1 on Amazon.com sales charts shortly after its release in the summer of 2016.

Carter resides in Denison, Texas where he continues to work at In Triumph and works on upcoming books on a variety of topics.

Also Available From

WordCrafts Press

Before History Dies
by Jacob M. Carter

The RipTide
by Jacob M. Carter

Why I Failed in the Music Business
and how NOT to follow in my footsteps
by Steve Grossman

Aerobics for the Mind
by Michael Potts, PhD

Confounding the Wise
by Dan Kulp

A Scarlet Cord of Hope
by Sheryl Griffin

Uncommon Core
by Pauline Hawkins

www.wordcrafts.net

www.ingramcontent.com/pod-product-compliance
Lightning Source LLC
Chambersburg PA
CBHW071538080526
44588CB00011B/1718